CHOCOLATE

CHOCOLATE

southwater

This edition published by Southwater

Distributed in the UK by
The Manning Partnership
Batheaston, Bath BA1 7RL, UK
tel. (0044) 01225 852 727
fax. (0044) 01225 852 852

Distributed in the USA by
Ottenheimer Publishing
5 Park Center Court
Suite 300
Owing Mills MD 2117-5001, USA
tel. (001) 410 902 9100
fax. (001) 410 902 7210

Distributed in Australia by
Sandstone Publishing
56 John Street, Leichhardt
New South Wales 2040, Australia
tel. (0061) 2 9552 3815
fax. (0061) 2 9552 1538

Distributed in New Zealand by
Five Mile Press NZ
Unit 3/46a Taharoto Road, PO Box 33-1071
Takapuna, Auckland 9, New Zealand
tel. (0064) 9 486 1925
fax. (0064) 9 486 1454

Southwater is an imprint of
Anness Publishing Limited
© 1996, 2000 Anness Publishing Limited
1 3 5 7 9 10 8 6 4 2

Publisher: Joanna Lorenz
Senior Cookery Editor: Linda Fraser
Cookery Editor: Anne Hildyard
Designer: Lisa Tai
Illustrations: Anna Koska
Photographers: Karl Adamson, Edward Allwright, Steve Baxter,
James Duncan, Amanda Heywood and Don Last
Recipes: Catherine Atkinson, Alex Barker, Frances Cleary, Christine France, Sarah Gates, Shirley Gill, Patricia
Lousada, Norma MacMillan and Elizabeth Wolf-Cohen
Food for photography: Carla Capalbo, Frances Cleary, Carole Handslip, Wendy Lee, Jane Stevenson and
Elizabeth Wolf-Cohen,
Stylists: Madeleine Brehaut, Maria Kelly, Blake Minton and Fiona Tillet

Previously published as *Cooking with Chocolate*
Printed in Singapore
Typeset by MC Typeset Ltd, Rochester, Kent

For all recipes, quantities are given in both metric and imperial measures and,
where appropriate, measures are also given in standard cups and spoons.
Follow one set, but not a mixture, because they are not interchangeable.

Contents

$\mathcal{I}$NTRODUCTION

Wicked, decadent, rich, mouth-watering, "to die for". Guess which one ingredient crops up in the dishes described? If you need some more clues, try "a chocoholic's delight" or "a chocolate lover's dream come true". Yes, it's chocolate, one of the most emotive of ingredients; and certainly one of the most popular.

But the chocolate which we know and love nowadays has not always been consumed in this form. When Cortés and his conquistadors were treated to a banquet by the Aztec emperor Montezuma in 1519, they were given cold chocolate to drink in sumptuous gold goblets. This rather bitter, spicy drink was completely different from our hot drinking chocolate. It was thickened by maize and flavoured with vanilla and ginger and often chilli and turmeric. Nowadays breakfast in Mexico is likely to be washed down with a drink of sweetened hot chocolate flavoured with spices such as cinnamon and ginger. The word itself is derived from *xocolatl*, the Aztec word for their cocoa-based drink.

The trade with Europe began to develop during the latter part of the 16th century, as a result of the Spanish conquests in Mexico and Central America. During the 17th century, chocolate houses became

extremely fashionable among the wealthy in large cities such as Florence, Brussels, Vienna and London.

The drink was, however, no longer a cold, bitter drink but a hot, sweetened drink. It was not until the mid 1800's that chocolate lost some of its exclusive tag and became available to the masses. This followed

Van Houten's invention, in his native Holland in 1828, of a machine to extract the cocoa butter from the bean. There was a surge of interest in Britain, advanced by the famous Quaker families, the Frys, Rowntrees, Terrys and Cadburys. Their primary aim was to promote drinking chocolate as a healthier alternative to gin! But when Joseph Fry discovered, in 1847, that by adding chocolate liquor and sugar to cocoa butter, a solid, eating chocolate was formed, the chocolate bar was born. Understandably, it did not take long for chocolate in the form of food, rather than drink, to catch on.

And it has caught on, all over the world.

In this delectable book, you will find chocolate blending with such different ingredients as chestnuts, dates, blueberries, apricots and brandy. One of the most versatile of sweet ingredients, whether it is dark, milk or white chocolate, it serves to give pleasure and has come to signify sharing and love. It is one of the most-prized of foods. Little wonder the Aztecs called it "food of the gods".

Sue Lawrence

TYPES OF CHOCOLATE

COCOA POWDER

The residue left after the cocoa butter has been pressed from the ground, roasted beans. Sweetened cocoa is used for drinks. In Britain, this is blended with powdered milk and called "drinking chocolate". Unsweetened cocoa powder is used for baking.

TYPES OF BLOCK CHOCOLATE

The quality of block chocolate varies according to the quantity of cocoa butter it contains. Most types have around 27 per cent. The higher the proportion of cocoa butter, the more easily it melts.

MILK, SWEET OR EATING CHOCOLATE

Rarely used for cooking, this chocolate tastes good because of added sugar and condensed or powdered milk.

PLAIN OR COOKING CHOCOLATE

A pleasant-tasting chocolate because it contains some sugar, it is often used for cooking. The cocoa butter content varies depending on the particular brand.

UNSWEETENED CHOCOLATE

Unsweetened with a high proportion of cocoa butter, this is used mainly for baking.

WHITE CHOCOLATE

This is creamy in colour and texture as it does not contain any cocoa solids but does contain cocoa butter and sugar. It does not set as firmly as milk and dark chocolate. It is called "white coating" in the US.

COUVERTURE CHOCOLATE

Used by professional cooks because it melts smoothly, it has a high cocoa butter content (up to 50 per cent) but needs tempering. Also called dipping or coating chocolate, it comes in dark, milk and white options.

CHOCOLATE DROPS, STRANDS AND BUTTONS

Drops and buttons are used in baking, and strands are sprinkled over iced cakes.

ORGANIC CHOCOLATE

This is made without chemical additives.

Cocoa powder

Organic chocolate

White couverture chocolate

Plain chocolate
drops

Milk couverture chocolate

Plain chocolate curls

White chocolate
curls

White chocolate

Milk chocolate

Chocolate strands

Plain chocolate

Milk chocolate drops

Plain couverture
chocolate

White chocolate
drops

White chocolate buttons

$\mathcal{B}$ASIC $\mathcal{T}$ECHNIQUES

MELTING CHOCOLATE

When melting chocolate for use in recipes, all equipment must be completely dry. Do not cover during or after melting because any water or condensation could cause the chocolate to seize or stiffen.

Of the methods shown below, the double boiler method is the most traditional and reliable. The direct heat method is a little more tricky and best used when another ingredient such as cream, milk or butter is added.

Melting by microwaving is fast but must be checked at 5–10-second intervals as the chocolate could quite easily burn.

Fill to half way the lower part of the double boiler with water and bring it to simmering point. Place the chopped or broken chocolate in the top part. With the heat low, melt the chocolate slowly, stirring to distribute the heat evenly. Remove the bowl as soon as the chocolate is fully melted. If you do not have a double boiler, place a small heatproof bowl over a saucepan so that it sits above the water and melt the chocolate as above.

Place the chocolate with the milk, cream or butter in a heavy-based saucepan and melt over a low heat, stirring constantly. Do not leave the chocolate unattended and take it off the heat as soon as it is smooth.

For 115g/4oz dark or semisweet chocolate, place the broken-up chocolate in a microwave-safe bowl and microwave on medium power (50 per cent) for about 2 minutes. For the same amount of milk or white chocolate, melt on low power (30 per cent) for about 2 minutes. These are approximate times based on a 650–700 watt oven. Ovens vary so check the chocolate halfway through – it will look shiny but still in shape.

TEMPERING CHOCOLATE

When using couverture chocolate, or if preparing to make moulded chocolates, coatings or sophisticated decorations, it must be tempered for good results. This is a procedure where the chocolate is gently heated and cooled to stabilize the cocoa solids and butter which would otherwise cause cooked chocolate to "bloom" – become cloudy or dull in appearance. Tempering makes the chocolate shiny and easy to work. Chocolate for general baking does not require tempering.

1 Melt the couverture chocolate until it has reached a temperature of 45°C/110°F. Stir well until it is melted and smooth.

2 Pour out three-quarters on to a marble slab. Using a palette knife, scrape into a pool and spread out again. Work for 3–5 minutes then mix with the remaining chocolate. Reheat to 29°C/85°F before use.

COATING OR DIPPING

For recipes that require coating or dipping such as sweets, truffles, caramels, dried and fresh fruit and biscuits, use tempered couverture chocolate for the best results. If couverture chocolate is difficult to find, use plain chocolate but chill immediately to prevent a bloom forming on the surface.

Melt the chocolate then pour it into a bowl for dipping. The temperature should be about 46°C/115°F. Use a skewer or fondue fork to lower the sweet or fruit into the chocolate. Turn to coat and lift out, tapping to remove excess. Place the dipped sweet or fruit on a non-stick baking sheet until dry. Chill immediately.

DECORATING WITH CHOCOLATE

QUICK CHOCOLATE CURLS

These are used as a simple decoration on a variety of cakes and desserts. For best effect, make a large amount and pile them on in an elegant profusion. Easy to make, they can be stored for weeks in an airtight container.

1 Bring a bar of chocolate to room temperature. Using a potato peeler with a swivel blade, peel the edge of the chocolate bar towards you, making small curls. Let them fall on to a sheet of greaseproof paper.

2 Use a skewer or cocktail stick to transfer the curls on to the dessert singly, or use a cool knife to slide a whole line of curls. Do not touch the curls with fingers as they will melt easily.

CHUNKY CHOCOLATE CURLS

These add a professional look to desserts and cakes, yet are fairly easy to make with a swivel-bladed peeler. Work quickly or the chocolate will have to be reheated.

1 Using tempered chocolate, pour it into a tin lined with non-stick baking paper, to produce a block about 2.5cm/1in thick. Chill until set.

2 Allow to come to room temperature, remove the chocolate block from the tin, then use a swivel-bladed peeler to make short chunky curls.

MAKING CHOCOLATE SHAPES

Chocolate shapes add an attractive finish to mousses and cakes. The simplest of all shapes to make is the triangle. You can also make squares or semi-circles using pastry cutters, or any decorative shape such as hearts or stars with small metal biscuit cutters. Use melted and tempered couverture chocolate for shiny and long-lasting results, but if this is not available, ordinary melted good quality dark or cooking chocolate is fine.

1 Pour melted chocolate on to a marble slab. Spread with a palette knife. Cool until firm.

2 With a sharp knife cut the chocolate into a rectangle, then cut into small squares and then triangles. Alternatively, use cutters to stamp out decorative shapes.

CHOCOLATE LEAVES

Making chocolate leaves requires a delicate touch but they are worth the effort because they will enhance any dessert or gâteau they decorate. Use fresh and non-toxic leaves that have good veins such as rose, bay or lemon leaves.

1 Wash and dry the leaves thoroughly before use. Melt the chocolate and with a pastry brush or spoon, coat the veined side of each leaf. Be careful not to get chocolate on the other side or it will be difficult to remove.

2 Place the coated leaves with the chocolate side up on a sheet of non-stick baking paper and leave to set.

With cool hands, peel back the leaf from the stem end. If not used immediately, store them in a cool place.

Using Chocolate

These simple, chocolate cups can be used as an elegant dessert or *petits fours* when filled with mousse, ice cream or chocolate ganache. Use small or medium paper cups or cases that are usually available from specialist kitchenware shops.

1 Melt the chocolate and, with a pastry brush, coat the inside of the cases with a layer of chocolate. Allow this to set. Repeat with a second layer. Leave to set.

2 With cool hands, carefully peel off the paper cases. They can be filled as required. Keep the chocolate cups cold until ready to serve.

SPICED MOCHA DRINK   Serves 4

A rich and warming drink that is not for weight watchers but tastes absolutely heavenly.

Chop or grate 175g/6oz of milk chocolate. Melt it in a double boiler with 120ml/4fl oz/½ cup of single cream, stirring well. When the mixture is blended, remove from the heat. Making sure the coffee and the chocolate are at the same temperature, stir in 750ml/1¼ pints/3 cups of hot black coffee and 1.5ml/¼ tsp of ground cinnamon. Beat with a small whisk until frothy. Serve it hot in tall glasses or mugs topped with a scoop of whipped cream. As an optional decoration, sprinkle with cocoa powder.

CULINARY USES

Chocolate has a reputation for being both an aphrodisiac and an energizer (it contains caffeine) and it is said to be a migraine-giver and extremely addictive too. Despite this, however, chocolate is very popular and is used in cooking in many ways: in drinks, desserts, confectionery, cakes, pastries, ganache, ice creams and sauces, often in combination with other flavours such as vanilla, cinnamon, nuts, coffee and orange. Chocolate is also found in some unusual dishes, such as Italian chocolate-flavoured pasta, served as a dessert, and the Mexican dish of *mole* – turkey, chillies and dark chocolate.

BUYING AND STORING

Always buy the best quality chocolate for cooking as this will give a smoother, richer result. The best chocolate has a higher cocoa butter content, for example couverture chocolate (with up to 50 per cent cocoa butter), which is used by professional bakers and confectioners but must be tempered before use.

Store chocolate in a dry, cool place away from sunlight and well wrapped to prevent it absorbing any other flavours. Store away from strong odours. Dark or cooking chocolate will keep for up to a year in dry, cool conditions. Milk chocolate can be kept for up to six months.

TIPS AND HINTS

• Chocolate must be melted very slowly as it can easily become overcooked and refuse to bind.

• When melting chocolate, care must be taken not to let any water into it or it may stiffen and become totally unworkable. If it does, correct this by stirring in one teaspoon at a time of fat such as cocoa butter, vegetable oil, vegetable shortening or clarified unsalted butter. Add and stir until it is smooth again.

• Chocolate that has developed a bloom in a fridge can still be melted and used in recipes but it is unsuitable for grating or making curls.

• If adding liquid to melted chocolate, make sure that they are both at the same temperature. If the chocolate is hotter than the liquid, the chocolate may become lumpy; if it is colder, the cocoa butter may separate out.

• When chopping or grating chocolate, a dry board, knife and grater must be used. Chill the chocolate before beginning and, on a warm day, it is a good idea if the utensils are also chilled first. You can use a food processor but care must be taken not to over-process as it may become sticky and clump together.

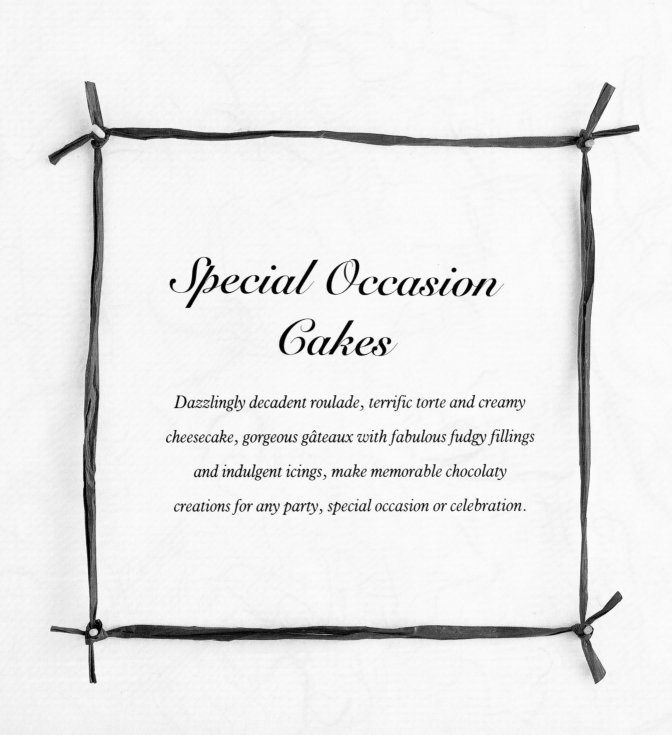

Special Occasion Cakes

Dazzlingly decadent roulade, terrific torte and creamy cheesecake, gorgeous gâteaux with fabulous fudgy fillings and indulgent icings, make memorable chocolaty creations for any party, special occasion or celebration.

CHOCOLATE DATE TORTE

A stunning cake that tastes wonderful. Rich and gooey – it's a chocoholic's delight!

Serves 8

200g/7oz/scant 1 cup fromage frais

200g/7oz/scant 1 cup mascarpone

5ml/1 tsp vanilla essence, plus a few
  extra drops

icing sugar, to taste

4 egg whites

115g/4oz/¹/₂ cup caster sugar

200g/7oz plain chocolate

175g/6oz/scant 1 cup Medjool dates,
  stoned and chopped

175g/6oz/1¹/₂ cups walnuts or pecan
  nuts, chopped

Preheat the oven to 180°C/350°F/Gas 4. Lightly grease and base-line a 20cm/8in springform cake tin. For the frosting, mix the fromage frais and mascarpone and add a few drops of vanilla essence and icing sugar to taste. Set aside. Whisk the egg whites in a bowl until they peak stiffly. Whisk in 30ml/2 tbsp of the caster sugar until thick and glossy, then fold in the rest. Chop 175g/6oz of the chocolate. Carefully fold into the meringue with the dates, nuts and 5ml/1 tsp of the vanilla essence. Pour into the tin, spread level and bake for 45 minutes, until risen. Cool in the tin for 10 minutes, then turn out on to a wire rack. Peel off the lining paper and leave until cold. Frost the top of the torte. Melt the remaining chocolate in a bowl over hot water. Spoon into a paper piping bag, snip off the top and drizzle the chocolate over the torte. Chill before serving.

17

FRENCH CHOCOLATE CAKE

This is typical of a French home-made cake – dense, dark and delicious. The texture is very different from a sponge cake and it is excellent served with cream or a fruit coulis.

Serves 10–12

150g/5oz/generous ½ cup caster sugar, plus extra for sprinkling

275g/10oz plain chocolate, chopped

175g/6oz/¾ cup unsalted butter, cut into pieces

10ml/2 tsp vanilla essence

5 eggs, separated

40g/1½oz/generous ¼ cup plain flour, sifted

pinch of salt

icing sugar, for dusting

whipped cream sweetened with icing sugar, to serve

Preheat the oven to 160°C/325°F/Gas 3. Generously grease a 24cm/9½in springform cake tin. Dust with a little sugar and tap out the excess.

Set aside 45ml/3 tbsp of the sugar. Place the chocolate, butter and remaining sugar in a large heavy-based pan and cook over a moderate heat until the chocolate and butter have melted and the sugar has dissolved. Remove the pan from the heat, stir in the vanilla essence and leave the mixture to cool slightly.

Beat the egg yolks into the chocolate mixture, beating well after each addition, then stir in the flour. In a large bowl, scrupulously clean and grease-free, and using clean beaters, whisk the egg whites, adding the salt, until they hold stiff peaks. Alternatively use an electric mixer. Sprinkle over the reserved sugar and beat until the whites are stiff and glossy. Beat one-third of the egg whites into the chocolate mixture, then carefully fold in the remaining whites.

Carefully pour the mixture into the prepared tin and tap the tin gently to release any air bubbles.

Bake for about 35–45 minutes until well risen or until a skewer inserted into the centre of the cake comes out clean. (If the cake appears to rise unevenly, rotate after 20–25 minutes.) Transfer the cake to a wire cooling rack, remove the sides of the tin and leave to cool completely. Remove the tin  base. Dust the cake with icing sugar and transfer to a serving plate. Serve with the whipped cream.

DEATH BY CHOCOLATE

There are many versions of this cake; this is a very rich one which is ideal for a large party.

Serves 18–20

225g/8oz cooking chocolate, chopped

115g/4oz/¹/₂ cup unsalted butter, diced

150ml/¹/₄ pint/²/₃ cup water

250g/9oz/generous 1 cup sugar

10ml/2 tsp vanilla essence

2 eggs, separated

150ml/¹/₄ pint/²/₃ cup buttermilk

365g/12¹/₂oz/3 cups plain flour

10ml/2 tsp baking powder

5ml/1 tsp bicarbonate of soda

pinch of cream of tartar

chocolate curls, raspberries and icing
  sugar, to decorate

For the fudge filling

450g/1lb cooking chocolate, chopped

225g/8oz/1 cup unsalted butter

85ml/3fl oz/¹/₃ cup brandy or rum

215g/7¹/₂oz/³/₄ cup raspberry preserve

For the chocolate ganache glaze

250ml/8fl oz/1 cup double cream

225g/8oz cooking chocolate, chopped

30ml/2 tbsp brandy

Preheat the oven to 180°C/350°F/Gas 4. Grease and base-line a 25cm/10in springform cake tin. Place the chocolate, butter and water in a pan and melt over a moderate heat. Remove from heat, beat in the sugar and vanilla and cool. Beat the egg yolks and then stir in the chocolate mixture. Fold in the buttermilk. Sift the flour, baking powder and bicarbonate into a bowl, then fold into the chocolate mixture. Whisk the egg whites and cream of tartar until they peak stiffly. Fold in the chocolate mixture. Pour the mixture into the tin. Bake for 45–50 minutes. Cool for 10 minutes on a wire rack. Run a knife around the edge of the tin. Remove the side. Invert the cake on to a wire rack, remove the base of the tin and cool. Wash the tin.

For the filling, melt the chocolate, butter and 60ml/4 tbsp brandy over moderate heat, stirring. Set aside to thicken. Cut the cake crossways into three. Melt the raspberry preserve and remaining brandy or rum, stirring. Spread thinly over each cake layer. Allow to set. Place the base cake layer back in the tin. Spread over half the filling, top with the second cake layer, then spread over the remaining filling and top with the top cake layer, preserve side down. Press the layers together, cover, and chill for 4–6 hours. Run a knife around the edge of the cake to loosen, unclip and remove the side of the tin. Set the cake on a wire rack over a baking sheet.

Bring the cream to the boil. Remove from heat and add the chocolate, stirring until melted. Stir in the brandy and strain into a bowl. Stand for 4–5 minutes to thicken. Working out towards the edge of the bowl, whisk the glaze until shiny. Pour over the cake using a palette knife to smooth the top and sides. Allow to set. Slide the cake on to a serving plate. Decorate with chocolate curls and raspberries and dust with icing sugar.

CHOCOLATE AND ORANGE ANGEL CAKE

This light-as-air sponge with its fluffy icing is virtually fat-free, yet tastes heavenly.

Serves 10

25g/1oz/¼ cup plain flour

15g/½oz/2 tbsp cocoa powder

15g/½oz/2 tbsp cornflour

pinch of salt

5 egg whites

2.5ml/½ tsp cream of tartar

115g/4oz/½ cup caster sugar

blanched and shredded rind of
  1 orange, to decorate

For the icing

200g/7oz/scant 1 cup caster sugar

1 egg white

Preheat the oven to 180°C/350°F/Gas 4. Sift the flour, cocoa powder, cornflour and salt together three times. In a large bowl, scrupulously clean and grease-free, whisk the egg whites until foamy. Add the cream of tartar, then whisk again until soft peaks form.

Gradually add the caster sugar to the egg whites a spoonful at a time, whisking after each addition. Sift a third of the flour and cocoa mixture over the meringue and gently fold in. Repeat, sifting and folding in the flour and cocoa mixture two more times.

Pour the mixture into a non-stick 20cm/8in ring mould and level the top. Bake in the oven for 35 minutes or until springy when lightly pressed. Turn upside-down on to a wire cooling rack. Allow to cool in the tin. Carefully ease out of the tin.

To make the icing, put the caster sugar in a pan with 75ml/5 tbsp cold water. Stir over a low heat until dissolved. Boil this syrup until it reaches a temperature of 120°C/250°F on a sugar thermometer, or when a drop of the syrup makes a soft ball when dropped into a cup of cold water. Remove from the heat immediately.

Whisk the egg white until it is stiff. Add the sugar syrup in a thin stream, whisking all the time. Continue to whisk until the icing mixture is very thick and fluffy.

Spread the icing over the top and sides of the cooled cake. Sprinkle the orange rind over the top of the cake and serve.

COOK'S TIP

Make sure you do not overbeat the egg whites. They should not be stiff but should form soft peaks, so that the air bubbles can expand during cooking and help the cake to rise.

CHOCOLATE NUT CAKE

There is a choice of nuts to use in this cake according to your preference.

Serves 6–8

cocoa powder, for dusting

175g/6oz plain chocolate, chopped into
    small pieces

115g/4oz/¹/₂ cup unsalted butter

225g/8oz/1 cup caster sugar

4 eggs, separated

115g/4oz/1 cup freshly ground unsalted
    macadamia nuts or almonds

25g/1oz/¹/₄ cup plain flour

pinch of cream of tartar (optional)

whipped cream sweetened with icing
    sugar, to serve

COOK'S TIP

*Beating egg whites should
always be the last step in
preparation of cakes or any
other recipes. Once they are
beaten, they should be folded
in at once, not left to stand.*

Preheat the oven to 160°C/325°F/Gas 3. Lightly grease and base-line a 23cm/9in springform cake tin. Dust with cocoa powder.

Place the chocolate and butter in a heavy-based pan and cook over moderate heat until melted. Leave the mixture to cool slightly. Beat together the sugar and egg yolks until pale and thick. Gently stir in the cooled chocolate mixture, nuts and flour until completely blended.

In a large bowl, clean and grease-free, whisk the egg whites until they peak stiffly. (If not using a copper bowl, add the cream of tartar when the whites are frothy.) Add one-quarter of the whites to the chocolate mixture and gently fold in using a rubber spatula. Add the remaining egg whites and fold them in gently but thoroughly.

Pour the mixture into the prepared tin. Bake for 1–1¼ hours. Cool in the tin for 10 minutes, then turn out on to a wire rack to cool completely. Dust with cocoa powder and serve with the whipped cream.

CHOCOLATE TRUFFLES

These truffles, like the prized fungi they resemble, are a Christmas speciality in France.

Makes 20–30

175ml/6fl oz/³⁄4 cup double cream

275g/10oz plain chocolate, chopped

25g/1oz/2 tbsp unsalted butter, cut into pieces

30–45ml/2–3 tbsp brandy (optional)

For the coatings

cocoa powder

finely chopped pistachios or hazelnuts

400g/14oz plain, milk or white chocolate, or a mixture

Place the cream in a pan and bring to the boil over moderate heat. Remove from the heat and add the chocolate, stirring until melted. Stir in the butter and the brandy, if using, then strain into a bowl and leave to cool. Cover and chill for 6–8 hours. Line a baking sheet with greaseproof paper. Using two teaspoons, form the mixture into 20–30 balls and place on the paper. Chill to harden. To coat the truffles, sift the cocoa powder into a small bowl, drop in one truffle at a time, and roll to coat well. Roll some truffles in finely chopped pistachios or hazelnuts. Freeze for 1 hour. To coat with chocolate, melt the plain, milk or white chocolate in a bowl over a pan of simmering water, stirring until melted, then allow to cool slightly. Using a fork, dip one truffle at a time into the chocolate, tapping the fork on the bowl edge to shake off the excess. Place on a baking sheet lined with non-stick baking paper and chill at once. If the chocolate thickens, reheat until smooth. Chill, well wrapped, for up to ten days.

CHOCOLATE CHEESECAKE

A luscious cheesecake prettily decorated using a paper doily.

Serves 12

450g/1lb plain chocolate, broken
*   into pieces*
115g/4oz/1/2 cup caster sugar
10ml/2 tsp vanilla essence
4 eggs
675g/11/2lb/23/8 cups cream cheese,
*   at room temperature*
30–45ml/2–3 tbsp icing sugar,
*   to decorate*

For the base

115g/4oz digestive biscuits, crushed
65g/21/2oz/5 tbsp butter or
*   margarine, melted*
30ml/2 tbsp grated plain chocolate
30ml/2 tbsp caster sugar

COOK'S TIP

For an all-chocolate cheesecake,
use finely crushed chocolate
wafers for the base.

Preheat the oven to 160°C/325°F/Gas 3. Lightly grease and base-line a 23–25cm/9–10in springform cake tin.

To make the base, mix together the crushed biscuits, melted butter or margarine, grated chocolate and caster sugar until thoroughly combined. Pat evenly over the bottom and up the sides of the prepared tin. (The base is intended to be thin.)

In a heatproof bowl set over a pan of barely simmering water, or in a double-boiler, melt the chocolate with the caster sugar. Remove the bowl from the heat and stir in the vanilla essence. Set aside and allow the mixture to cool briefly.

In another bowl, beat together the eggs and cream cheese until smooth and well combined. Gently stir in the cooled chocolate mixture until completely blended.

Pour the chocolate filling into the biscuit base. Bake for about 45 minutes or until the filling is set. Allow to cool in the tin on a wire cooling rack. Chill for at least 12 hours.

Transfer the cheesecake to a serving plate and remove the side of the tin. To decorate, lay a paper doily on the surface of the cake and sift the icing sugar evenly over the doily. With two hands, carefully lift off the doily to reveal the pattern.

CHOCOLATE CHESTNUT ROULADE

The glacé chestnuts could be dipped in melted plain chocolate for the decoration.

Serves 10–12

170g/6oz cooking chocolate, chopped
30ml/2 tbsp cocoa powder, sifted
50ml/2fl oz/¼ cup strong coffee
  or espresso
6 eggs, separated
90ml/6 tbsp caster sugar
pinch of cream of tartar
5ml/1 tsp vanilla essence
cocoa powder, for dusting
glacé chestnuts, to decorate

For the chestnut cream filling

475ml/16fl oz/2 cups double cream
30ml/2 tbsp rum or coffee-flavour
  liqueur
350g/12oz/1½ cups canned sweetened
  chestnut purée
115g/4oz cooking chocolate, grated

Preheat the oven to 180°C/350°F/Gas 4. Grease and line the base and sides of a 39 × 27 × 2.5cm/15½ × 10½ × 1in Swiss roll tin, allowing a 2.5cm/1in overhang. In a heatproof bowl set over a pan of simmering water, melt the chocolate until smooth. Set aside. Dissolve the cocoa in the coffee to make a smooth paste. Set aside. Beat the egg yolks with half the sugar until pale and thick, about 3–5 minutes. Slowly beat in the melted chocolate and cocoa-coffee paste until just blended. Beat the egg whites and cream of tartar until stiff peaks form. Sprinkle the sugar over the whites in two batches and beat until stiff and glossy; beat in the vanilla. Stir a spoonful of whites into the chocolate mixture, then fold in the remaining whites. Spoon into the tin. Bake for 20–25 minutes or until the cake springs back when touched. Dust a dish towel with cocoa powder. When the cake is done, turn out on to the towel immediately and remove the paper. Starting at a narrow end, roll cake and towel together Swiss roll style. Cool completely.

To make the filling, whip the cream and rum or liqueur until soft peaks form. Beat a spoonful of cream into the chestnut purée, then fold in the remaining cream and grated chocolate. Reserve a quarter of the chestnut cream mixture for decoration. Unroll the roulade and trim the edges. Spread the chestnut cream mixture to within 2.5cm/1in of the edge of the cake. Using the towel to lift the cake, gently re-roll the cake. Place the roulade seam-side down on a serving plate. Spread the reserved chestnut cream over the top of the roulade, and spoon some into a piping bag fitted with a medium star tip. Pipe rosettes down the sides and decorate with glacé chestnuts.

RICH CHOCOLATE CAKE

This dark, fudgy cake is easy to make, stores well and is a chocolate lover's dream come true.

Serves 14–16

225g/8oz/1 cup unsalted butter, cut
into pieces
250g/9oz plain chocolate, chopped
5 eggs
90g/3½oz/7 tbsp caster sugar, plus
15ml/1 tbsp and extra for sprinkling
15ml/1 tbsp cocoa powder
10ml/2 tsp vanilla essence
cocoa powder, for dusting
chocolate shavings, to decorate

Preheat the oven to 160°C/325°F/Gas 3. Lightly grease and base-line a 23cm/9in springform cake tin. Butter the paper and sprinkle with a little sugar, then tip out the excess.

The cake is baked in a *bain-marie*, so carefully wrap the base and sides of the tin with a double thickness of foil to prevent water leaking into the cake.

In a heatproof bowl set over a pan of barely simmering water, or in a double-boiler, melt the butter and chocolate. Beat the eggs with 90g/3½oz/ 7 tbsp of the sugar using an electric mixer.

Mix together the cocoa powder and 15ml/1 tbsp sugar and beat into the egg mixture until well blended. Beat in the vanilla essence, then slowly beat in the melted chocolate until well blended. Pour the mixture into the prepared tin and tap gently to release any air bubbles.

Place the cake tin in a roasting tin and pour in boiling water to come 2cm/¾in up the sides of the wrapped tin. Bake for 45–50 minutes or until the edge of the cake is set and the centre still soft (a skewer inserted 5cm/2in from the edge should come out clean). Lift the tin out of the water and remove the foil. Transfer to a wire cooling rack, remove the side of the tin and leave the cake to cool completely (the cake will sink a little in the centre).

Invert the cake on to the wire rack. Remove the base of the tin and the paper. Dust the cake liberally with cocoa powder and arrange the chocolate shavings around the edge. Slide the cake on to a serving plate.

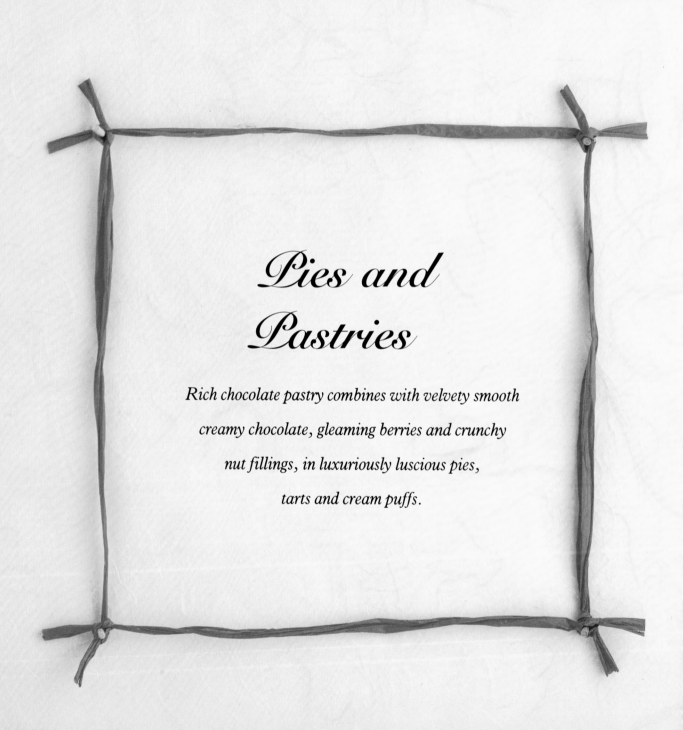

Pies and Pastries

Rich chocolate pastry combines with velvety smooth

creamy chocolate, gleaming berries and crunchy

nut fillings, in luxuriously luscious pies,

tarts and cream puffs.

VELVET MOCHA CREAM PIE

The texture of this pie is as smooth and rich as velvet.

Serves 8

10ml/2 tsp instant espresso coffee

30ml/2 tbsp hot water

350ml/12fl oz/1½ cups
   whipping cream

175g/6oz plain chocolate

25g/1oz cooking chocolate

120ml/4fl oz/½ cup whipped cream
   and chocolate-coated coffee beans,
   to decorate

For the base

150g/5oz chocolate wafers, crushed

30ml/2 tbsp caster sugar

65g/2½oz/5 tbsp butter, melted

To make the base, mix the crushed chocolate wafers and sugar together, then stir in the melted butter. Press the mixture evenly over the base and side of a 23cm/9in pie dish. Chill until firm.

In a bowl, dissolve the coffee in the hot water and set aside. Pour the cream into a mixing bowl set in hot water to warm it. In a heatproof bowl set over a pan of simmering water, melt both types of chocolate. Remove from the heat when nearly melted and stir to continue melting. Set the base of the pan in cool water to reduce the temperature. Be careful not to splash any water on the chocolate. Whip the cream. Add the dissolved coffee and whip until the cream just holds its shape. When the chocolate is at room temperature, fold it gently into the cream. Pour into the chilled biscuit base and chill until firm. To serve, pipe a ring of whipped cream rosettes around the edge, then place a coffee bean in the centre of each.

CHOCOLATE CHIP PECAN PIE

A handsome pie suitable for an elegant dinner party dessert.

Serves 8–10

175g/6oz/1¼ cups plain flour

15ml/1 tbsp caster sugar

2.5ml/½ tsp salt

115g/4oz/½ cup unsalted butter, cut
  into small pieces

120ml/4fl oz/½ cup iced water

For the filling

75g/3oz unsweetened
  chocolate, chopped

50g/2oz/4 tbsp butter, cut into pieces

3 eggs

165g/5½oz/scant ¾ cup soft light
  brown sugar

175ml/6fl oz/¾ cup corn or
  glucose syrup

15ml/1 tbsp vanilla essence

225g/8oz/2 cups pecan halves

75g/3oz/½ cup plain chocolate drops

To make the pastry, blend the flour, sugar and salt in a food processor or blender. Add the butter and process for 15–20 seconds until the mixture resembles coarse crumbs. With machine running, add iced water until the dough begins to stick together; do not allow it to form a ball or the pastry will be tough. Shape into a flat disc, wrap in greaseproof paper and chill for 1 hour. Butter a 23cm/9in tart tin. Soften the dough for 10–15 minutes at room temperature. On a floured surface, roll it out into a 30cm/12in round, 3mm/⅛in thick. Use to line the tart tin. Trim the pastry even with the rim of the tin; using fingers, flatten to the rim of the tin. Re-roll trimmings to a long rectangle and cut thin strips about 5mm/¼in wide. Plait three strips together. Repeat until you have enough to fit around the pie edge. Brush the pastry edge with water and press on the plaits. Prick the base with a fork. Chill for 30 minutes. Preheat the oven to 200°C/400°F/Gas 6. Line the pastry case with non-stick baking paper and fill with dry beans. Bake for 5 minutes, lift out the paper and beans and bake for 5 more minutes. Remove to a wire rack. Lower the oven temperature to 190°C/375°F/Gas 5.

For the filling, melt the chocolate and butter in a pan over a low heat, stirring until smooth. Set aside to cool slightly. Beat the eggs with the sugar, syrup and vanilla. Slowly beat in the melted chocolate. Arrange the pecan halves and the chocolate drops over the base of the pastry. Place the tart tin on a baking sheet and pour the chocolate mixture into the pastry case. Bake for 35–45 minutes, until the chocolate mixture is set. If the pastry edge begins to brown too quickly, cover with strips of foil. Put the pie on a wire rack to cool. Serve warm or chilled.

RICH CHOCOLATE-BERRY TART

Raspberries, blackberries, alpine strawberries, boysenberries or loganberries may be used in this tart.

Serves 10

115g/4oz/½ cup unsalted
  butter, softened
115g/4oz/½ cup caster sugar
2.5ml/½ tsp salt
15ml/1 tbsp vanilla essence
50g/2oz/½ cup cocoa powder
215g/7½oz/1½ cups plain flour
450g/1lb fresh berries, for topping

For the ganache filling

450ml/16fl oz/2 cups double cream
150g/5oz/½ cup seedless blackberry or
  raspberry preserve
225g/8oz cooking chocolate, chopped
25g/1oz/2 tbsp unsalted butter, diced

For the sauce

225g/8oz fresh or frozen blackberries
  or raspberries, thawed
15ml/1 tbsp lemon juice
30ml/2 tbsp caster sugar
30ml/2 tbsp blackberry- or raspberry-
  flavour liqueur

To make the pastry, process the butter, sugar, salt and vanilla in a food processor or blender until creamy. Add the cocoa and process for 1 minute; scrape the side of the bowl. Add the flour all at once and using the pulse action, process for 10–15 seconds, until just blended. Place a piece of clear film on the work surface and turn out the dough on to it. Use clear film to help shape the dough into a flat disc. Wrap tightly and chill for 1 hour.

Grease a 23cm/9in tart tin with removable base. Soften the dough for 10 minutes at room temperature. Roll it out between two sheets of clear film to a 28cm/11in round, 5mm/¼in thick. Peel off the top sheet of clear film and invert the dough into the tin. Ease it in and remove the clear film.

With floured fingers, press the dough on to the base and side of the tin, trim off any excess and prick the base with a fork. Chill for 1 hour. Preheat oven to 180°C/350°F/Gas 4. Line the pastry case with non-stick baking paper and fill with dry beans. Bake for 10 minutes. Lift out the paper and beans and bake for 5 minutes more. Remove to a wire rack to cool completely.

To make the filling, bring the cream and preserve to the boil in a pan over a moderate heat. Remove from the heat and add the chocolate all at once, stirring until melted and smooth. Stir in the butter and strain into the cooled pastry case, smoothing the top. Cool the tart completely.

To make the sauce, combine the berries, lemon juice and sugar in a food processor and process until smooth. Strain into a small bowl and add the liqueur. If the sauce is too thick, thin with a little water.

To serve, remove the tart from the tin. Place on a serving plate and arrange the berries on the top of the tart. With a pastry brush, brush the berries with a little of the sauce to glaze. Serve the remaining sauce separately.

CHOCOLATE APRICOT LINZER TART

To dust in stripes, place baking paper strips on the tart before dusting with icing sugar.

Serves 10–12

70g/2¹/₂oz/generous ¹/₂ cup whole
   blanched almonds
115g/4oz/²/₃ cup caster sugar
215g/7¹/₂oz/generous 1¹/₂ cups
   plain flour
30ml/2 tbsp cocoa powder
5ml/1 tsp ground cinnamon
2.5ml/¹/₂ tsp salt
5ml/1 tsp grated orange rind
225g/8oz/1 cup unsalted butter, diced
30–45ml/2–3 tbsp iced water
75g/3oz/¹/₂ cup plain chocolate drops
icing sugar, for dusting

For the apricot filling

350g/12oz ready-to-eat dried apricots
120ml/4fl oz/¹/₂ cup orange juice
175ml/6fl oz/³/₄ cup water
45ml/3 tbsp granulated sugar
30ml/2 tbsp apricot preserve
2.5ml/¹/₂ tsp ground cinnamon
2.5ml/¹/₂ tsp almond essence

To make the filling, bring the apricots, orange juice and water to the boil over moderate heat. Lower the heat and simmer for 15–20 minutes until the liquid is absorbed, stirring frequently. Stir in the sugar, apricot preserve, cinnamon and almond essence. Press the mixture through a strainer into a bowl, cool, then cover and chill.

To make the pastry, butter a 28cm/11in tart tin with removable base. In a food processor or blender, finely grind the almonds with half the sugar. Sift the flour, cocoa, remaining sugar, cinnamon and salt into a bowl. Add to the food processor and blend. Add the orange rind and butter and process for 20 seconds. Add 30ml/2 tbsp iced water and using the pulse action, process until the dough just begins to stick together. If the dough appears too dry, add more iced water, little by little, until it holds together.

Knead the dough until just blended. Divide in half. Press half the dough on to the base and side of tin. Prick base with a fork. Chill for 30 minutes. Roll out remaining dough between two sheets of clear film to a 28cm/11in round. Slide it on to a baking sheet and chill for 30 minutes.

Preheat the oven to 180°C/350°F/Gas 4. Spread the filling on to the base. Sprinkle with chocolate drops. Slide the dough round on to a floured surface and cut into 1cm/¹/₂in wide strips.

Make a lattice pattern with the strips over the filling. Press the ends to the edge of the tart and trim. Press down on each side of each crossing to accentuate the lattice effect.

Bake for 35–40 minutes until the top of the pastry is set and the filling bubbles. Cool on a wire rack to room temperature. To serve, remove the side of the tin and dust icing sugar over the top pastry strips.

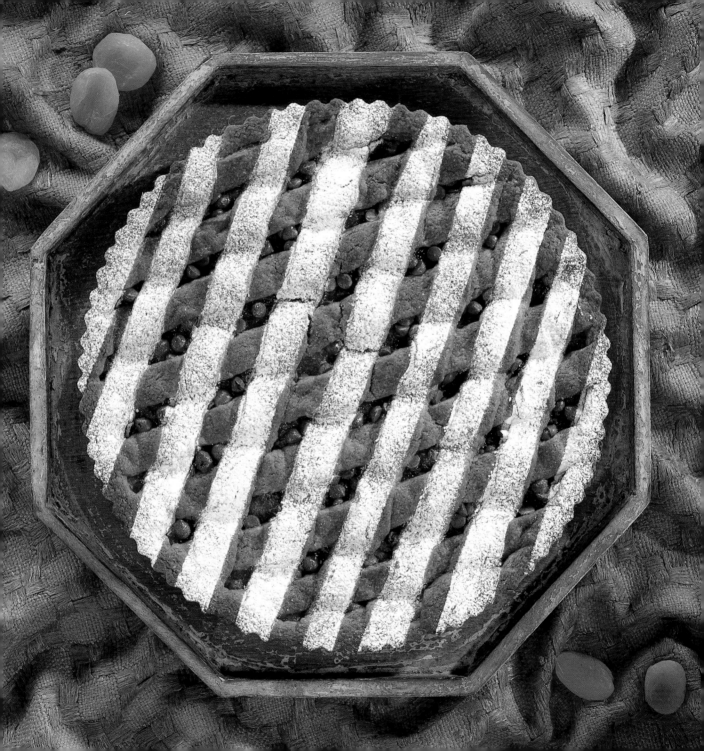

CHOCOLATE PROFITEROLES

This mouth-watering dessert is served in cafés throughout France. Sometimes the profiteroles are filled with whipped cream instead of ice cream, but they are always drizzled with chocolate sauce.

Serves 4–6
275g/10oz plain chocolate
120ml/4fl oz/½ cup warm water
750ml/1¼ pints/3 cups vanilla
  ice cream

For the profiteroles
75g/3oz/¾ cup plain flour
1.5ml/¼ tsp salt
pinch of freshly grated nutmeg
175ml/6fl oz/¾ cup water
75g/3oz/6 tbsp unsalted butter, cut
  into 6 pieces
3 eggs

Preheat the oven to 200°C/400°F/Gas 6 and lightly grease a large baking sheet. To make the profiteroles, sift together the flour, salt and nutmeg. In a pan, bring the water and butter to the boil. Remove from the heat and add the dry ingredients all at once. Beat with a wooden spoon for about 1 minute until well blended and the mixture starts to pull away from the sides of the pan. Set the pan over a low heat and cook the mixture for about 2 minutes, beating constantly. Remove from the heat.

Beat one egg in a small bowl and set aside. Add the remaining eggs, one at a time, to the flour mixture, beating well after each addition. Add the beaten egg by teaspoonfuls until the dough is smooth and shiny; it should pull away and fall slowly when dropped from a spoon.

Using a tablespoon, drop the dough on to the baking sheet in 12 mounds. Bake for 25–30 minutes until the pastry is well risen and browned. Turn off the oven, open the door, and leave the profiteroles to cool.

To make the sauce, place the chocolate and water in a double-boiler or in a bowl placed over a pan of hot water and leave to melt, stirring occasionally. Keep warm until ready to serve, or reheat, over simmering water.

Split the profiteroles in half and put a small scoop of ice cream in each. Arrange on a serving platter or divide among individual plates. Pour the chocolate sauce over the top and serve at once.

Biscuits and Bakes

Crisp and crunchy cookies, simply gorgeous gooey

brownies, fabulous fruity muffins, and rich gingery

florentines are mouth-watering chocolaty treats — totally

irresistible and satisfying at any time of day.

CHOCOLATE FUDGE BROWNIES

The ultimate tea-time treat, brownies are a firm family favourite.

Makes 12

175g/6oz/³/4 cup butter
40g/1¹/2oz/generous ¹/2 cup
  cocoa powder
2 eggs, lightly beaten
175g/6oz/³/4 cup soft light brown sugar
2.5ml/¹/2 tsp vanilla essence
115g/4oz/1 cup chopped pecan nuts
50g/2oz/¹/2 cup self-raising flour

For the frosting

115g/4oz plain chocolate
25g/1oz/2 tbsp butter
15ml/1 tbsp soured cream

Preheat the oven to 180°C/350°F/Gas 4. Grease and base-line a 20cm/8in square, shallow cake tin. Melt the butter in a pan and stir in the cocoa.

Beat together the eggs, sugar and vanilla essence in a bowl, then stir in the cooled cocoa mixture with the nuts. Sift over the flour and fold in.

Pour the mixture into the prepared tin and bake for 30–35 minutes, until risen. Remove from the oven (the mixture will still be quite soft and wet, but it cooks further while cooling) and leave to cool in the tin.

To make the frosting, melt the chocolate and butter together in a pan and remove from the heat. Beat in the soured cream until smooth and glossy. Leave to cool slightly and then spread over the top of the brownies. When the frosting is set, cut into 12 pieces.

CHEWY CHOCOLATE COOKIES

Make two batches of these cookies at a time – they will disappear very quickly!

Makes 18

4 egg whites

275g/10oz/2½ cups icing sugar

115g/4oz cocoa powder

30ml/2 tbsp plain flour

5ml/1 tsp instant coffee powder

15ml/1 tbsp water

115g/4oz/1 cup walnuts,
finely chopped

Preheat the oven to 180°C/350°F/Gas 4. Line two baking sheets with greaseproof paper and grease the paper.

Beat the egg whites until frothy with an electric mixer. Sift the sugar, cocoa, flour, and coffee into the whites. Add the water and continue beating on low speed to blend, then on high for a few minutes until the mixture thickens. With a rubber spatula, fold in the walnuts.

Place generous tablespoonfuls of the mixture 2.5cm/1in apart on the prepared baking sheets. Bake for 12–15 minutes until firm and cracked on top but soft on the inside. Using a metal spatula, transfer to a wire rack to cool.

COOK'S TIP

If wished, add 75g/3oz/½ cup chocolate drops to the cookie dough along with the nuts.

CHOCOLATE BLUEBERRY MUFFINS

Paper cases not only make for easier washing up, but they also keep the muffins fresher.

Makes 12

115g/4oz/¹/₂ cup butter

75g/3oz unsweetened
*   chocolate, chopped*

200g/7oz/1 cup granulated sugar

1 egg, lightly beaten

250ml/8fl oz/1 cup buttermilk

10ml/2 tsp vanilla essence

225g/8oz/2 cups plain flour

5ml/1 tsp bicarbonate of soda

175g/6oz/1 cup fresh or frozen
*   blueberries, thawed*

25g/1oz cooking chocolate, melted

Preheat the oven to 190°C/375°F/Gas 5. Melt the butter and chocolate in a pan over a moderate heat until smooth, stirring frequently. Remove from the heat to cool slightly.

Stir in the sugar, egg, buttermilk and vanilla essence. Gently fold in the flour and bicarbonate of soda until just blended. (Do not overblend; the mixture may be lumpy with some unblended flour.) Fold in the berries.

Drop paper cases into a 12-cup muffin tin. Spoon in the mixture, filling to the top. Bake for 25–30 minutes until a skewer inserted in the centre comes out with just a few crumbs attached. Remove the muffins in their paper cases to a wire cooling rack immediately (if left in the tin they will go soggy). Drizzle with the melted chocolate and serve warm or cool.

BLACK AND WHITE GINGER FLORENTINES

These delicious florentines can be stored in an airtight container in the fridge for up to one week.

Makes about 30

120ml/4fl oz/½ cup double cream

50g/2oz/¼ cup unsalted butter

90g/3½oz/7 tbsp granulated sugar

30ml/2 tbsp honey

150g/5oz/1¼ cups flaked almonds

40g/1½oz/⅓ cup plain flour

2.5ml/½ tsp ground ginger

50g/2oz/⅓ cup diced candied
  orange peel

65g/2½oz/½ cup diced stem ginger

50g/2oz plain chocolate, chopped

150g/5oz cooking chocolate, chopped

150g/5oz fine quality white
  chocolate, chopped

Preheat the oven to 180°C/350°F/Gas 4. Lightly grease two large baking sheets. (Non-stick sheets are ideal for these caramel-like cookies.) Stir the cream, butter, sugar and honey in a pan over a moderate heat until the sugar dissolves. Bring the mixture to the boil, stirring constantly. Remove from the heat and stir in the almonds, flour and ground ginger until well blended. Stir in the orange peel, stem ginger and chopped plain chocolate.

Drop teaspoonfuls of mixture on to the prepared sheets at least 7.5cm/3in apart. Spread each round as thinly as possible with the back of the spoon.

Bake for 8–10 minutes or until the edges are golden brown and the biscuits are bubbling. Do not underbake or they will be sticky, but be careful not to overbake as the high sugar and fat content allows them to burn easily. Continue baking in batches. If you wish, use a 7.5cm/3in biscuit cutter to neaten the edges of the florentines while on the baking sheets. Remove the baking sheets to a wire cooling rack for 10 minutes. Then, with a metal palette knife, remove the biscuits to a wire rack to cool completely.

In a small pan over a very low heat, heat the cooking chocolate, stirring frequently, until melted and smooth. Cool slightly. In a heatproof bowl set over a pan of simmering water or in a double-boiler, melt the white chocolate until smooth, stirring frequently. Remove top of double-boiler from base and cool for about 5 minutes, stirring occasionally until slightly thickened.

Using a small metal palette knife, spread half the florentines with the cooking chocolate on the flat side of each biscuit, swirling to create a decorative surface, and place on a wire rack, chocolate side up. Spread remaining florentines with the melted white chocolate and place on rack, chocolate side up. Chill for 10–15 minutes to set completely.

Hot Puddings

Rich and dark, creamy white, and simple milk chocolate

make delicious desserts, sensational soufflés, a wonderful

hot chocolate cake and an almondy peach pudding

that is sheer indulgence.

CHOCOLATE AMARETTI PEACHES

Quick and easy to prepare, this delicious dessert can also be made with fresh nectarines or apricots.

Serves 4

115g/4oz amaretti biscuits, crushed
50g/2oz plain chocolate, chopped
grated rind of ½ orange
15ml/1 tbsp clear honey
1.5ml/¼ tsp ground cinnamon
1 egg white, lightly beaten
4 firm, ripe peaches
150ml/¼ pint/⅔ cup white wine
15ml/1 tbsp caster sugar
whipped cream, to serve

Preheat the oven to 190°C/375°F/Gas 5. Mix together the crushed amaretti biscuits, chocolate, orange rind, honey and cinnamon in a bowl. Add the beaten egg white and stir to bind the mixture together.

Halve and stone the peaches and fill the cavities with the chocolate mixture, mounding it up slightly.

Arrange the stuffed peaches in a lightly buttered, shallow ovenproof dish which will just hold the fruit comfortably. Pour the wine into a measuring jug and stir in the sugar.

Pour the wine mixture around the peaches. Bake for 30–40 minutes, until the peaches are tender. Serve at once with a little of the cooking juices spooned over and the whipped cream.

HOT CHOCOLATE CAKE

This is wonderfully wicked, either hot as a pudding served with a white chocolate sauce, or cold as a cake. The basic cake freezes well – thaw, then warm in the microwave before serving.

Makes 10–12 slices

200g/7oz/generous 1¾ cups self-raising
  wholemeal flour
25g/1oz/¼ cup cocoa powder
pinch of salt
175g/6oz/¾ cup soft margarine
175g/6oz/¾ cup soft light brown sugar
few drops of vanilla essence
4 eggs
75g/3oz white chocolate,
  roughly chopped
chocolate leaves and curls, to decorate

For the white chocolate sauce
75g/3oz white chocolate
150ml/¼ pint/⅔ cup single cream
30–45ml/2–3 tbsp milk

Preheat the oven to 160°C/325°F/Gas 3. Sift the flour, cocoa and salt into a bowl, adding back in the wholemeal flakes from the sieve.

In another bowl, cream the margarine, sugar and vanilla essence together until light and fluffy, then gently beat in one egg.

Gradually stir in the remaining eggs, one at a time, alternately folding in some of the flour. Then add the remaining flour and stir until all the flour mixture is blended in well.

Stir in the white chocolate and spoon into a 675–900g/1½–2lb loaf tin or an 18cm/7in greased cake tin. Bake for 30–40 minutes, or until just firm to the touch and shrinking away from the sides of the tin.

To make the sauce, heat the chocolate and cream very gently in a pan until the chocolate is melted. Remove from the heat. Gradually add the milk and stir until cool.

Serve the cake in generous slices, in a pool of sauce and decorated with chocolate leaves and curls.

HOT MOCHA SOUFFLES

These hot, sweet soufflés are easy to make, but don't be tempted to open the oven door during cooking!

Serves 4

50g/2oz/4 tbsp butter

40g/1½oz/⅓ cup plain flour

300ml/½ pint/1¼ cups milk

115g/4oz plain chocolate,
  finely chopped

15ml/1 tbsp instant coffee granules

90ml/6 tbsp caster sugar, plus extra for
  coating the dishes

5 eggs, separated

icing sugar, for dusting

Preheat the oven to 190°C/375°F/Gas 5. Generously butter four 300ml/ ½ pint/1¼ cup soufflé dishes, especially around the rims.

Sprinkle the dishes heavily with caster sugar and set aside. Melt the butter in a heavy-based pan. Stir in the flour and cook for 1 minute. Gradually add the milk and cook, stirring until thickened. Cook for 1–2 minutes, stirring.

Remove the pan from the heat and beat in the chocolate and coffee. Cool the chocolate mixture slightly, then beat in the sugar and egg yolks. Whisk the egg whites until stiff. Add a tablespoonful to the chocolate sauce and beat in to lighten the mixture. Gently fold in the rest.

Spoon the mixture into the dishes and bake for 20 minutes, or until well risen and just firm to the touch. Dust with icing sugar and serve immediately.

CHOCOLATE, DATE AND WALNUT PUDDING

Sticky dates and crunchy walnuts make this a pudding of wonderful contrasts.

Serves 4

25g/1oz/¼ cup chopped walnuts

25g/1oz/2 tbsp chopped dates

2 eggs

5ml/1 tsp vanilla essence

30ml/2 tbsp golden caster sugar

45ml/3 tbsp plain wholemeal flour

15ml/1 tbsp cocoa powder

30ml/2 tbsp milk

Preheat the oven to 180°C/350°F/Gas 4. Grease a 1.2 litre/2 pint/5 cup pudding basin and place a small circle of greaseproof or non-stick baking paper in the base. Spoon in the walnuts and dates.

Separate the eggs and place the yolks in a bowl, with the vanilla and sugar. Place over a pan of hot water and whisk until the mixture is thick and pale.

Sift the flour and cocoa into the mixture and fold them in with a metal spoon. Stir in the milk, to soften the mixture slightly. Whisk the egg whites until they hold soft peaks and fold them in.

Spoon the mixture into the basin and bake for 40–45 minutes, or until the pudding is well risen and firm to the touch. Run a knife around the pudding to loosen it from the basin, and then turn it out and serve immediately.

Cold Desserts

*Aromatic vanilla, coffee and spicy ginger make perfect
partners in delectable chilled chocolate desserts,
irresistible ice creams, marvellous marquises, creamy
custards and melt-in-the-mouth mousses and timbales.*

MOCHA CREAM POTS

The addition of coffee to this classic French dessert gives it an exotic touch.

Serves 8

15ml/1 tbsp instant coffee powder
475ml/16fl oz/2 cups milk
90ml/6 tbsp caster sugar
225g/8oz plain chocolate, chopped
10ml/2 tsp vanilla essence
30ml/2 tbsp coffee liqueur (optional)
7 egg yolks
whipped cream and crystallized
mimosa balls, to decorate

Preheat the oven to 160°C/325°F/Gas 3. Place eight 120ml/4fl oz/½ cup dessert cups or ramekins in a roasting tin.

Put the instant coffee into a pan and stir in the milk, then add the sugar and set the pan over a medium-high heat. Bring to the boil, stirring constantly, until the coffee and sugar have dissolved. Remove the pan from the heat and add the chocolate. Stir until smooth. Stir in the vanilla essence and coffee liqueur, if using.

Whisk the egg yolks lightly in a bowl. Slowly whisk in the chocolate mixture until blended, then strain into a large jug and divide equally among the cups or ramekins. Pour boiling water into the roasting tin to come halfway up the sides of the cups or ramekins.

Bake for about 30–35 minutes or until the custard is just set and a knife inserted into a custard comes out clean. Remove the cups or ramekins from the roasting tin and allow to cool. Place on a baking sheet, cover and chill completely. Decorate with whipped cream and crystallized mimosa balls.

CHILLED CHOCOLATE SLICE

This is a very rich family pudding, but it is also designed to use up the occasional leftover! You don't need to eat it in a rush – it keeps very well.

Serves 6–8

115g/4oz/½ cup butter, melted
225g/8oz ginger biscuits, finely crushed
50g/2oz/1 cup stale sponge cake crumbs
60–75ml/4–5 tbsp orange juice
115g/4oz/¼ cup stoned dates, warmed
25g/1oz/¼ cup finely chopped nuts
175g/6oz cooking chocolate
300ml/½ pint/1¼ cups
*   whipping cream*
grated chocolate and icing sugar,
*   to serve*

Mix together the butter and ginger biscuit crumbs, then pack around the base and side of an 18cm/7in loose-based flan tin. Chill.

Put the cake crumbs into a large bowl with the orange juice and leave to soak. Mash the warm dates thoroughly and blend into the cake crumbs along with the nuts.

Melt the chocolate with 45–60ml/3–4 tbsp of the cream. Softly whip the rest of the cream, then fold in the melted chocolate.

Stir the cream and chocolate mixture into the crumbs and mix well. Pour into the biscuit case, mark into portions and leave to set. Scatter over the grated chocolate and dust with icing sugar. Serve cut in wedges.

CHOCOLATE VANILLA TIMBALES

A light dessert, ideal for serving after a rich main course at a dinner party.

Serves 6

350ml/12fl oz/1½ cups milk

30ml/2 tbsp cocoa powder

2 eggs

5ml/1 tsp vanilla essence

45ml/3 tbsp granulated sugar

15ml/1 tbsp/1 sachet powdered gelatine

45ml/3 tbsp hot water

mint sprigs, to decorate

For the sauce

120ml/4fl oz/½ cup Greek-style yogurt

2.5ml/½ tsp vanilla essence

extra cocoa powder, to sprinkle

Place the milk and cocoa in a pan and stir until boiling. Separate the eggs and beat the egg yolks with the vanilla and sugar until the mixture is pale and smooth. Pour in the chocolate milk, beating well.

Return the mixture to the pan and stir constantly over a gentle heat, without boiling, until it is slightly thickened and smooth. Dissolve the gelatine in the hot water and then quickly stir it into the milk mixture. Let it cool until it is on the point of setting.

Whisk the egg whites until they hold soft peaks. Fold them quickly into the milk mixture. Spoon the timbale into six moulds and chill until set.

To serve, run a knife around the edge, dip the moulds quickly into hot water and turn out the chocolate timbales on to serving plates. To make the sauce, stir together the yogurt and vanilla and spoon on to the plates. Sprinkle with cocoa and decorate with a mint sprig.

CHOCOLATE LOAF WITH COFFEE SAUCE

This type of chocolate dessert is popular in many French restaurants. Sometimes the loaf is encased in sponge, but this version is easier and it can be served cold or frozen.

Serves 6–8

175g/6oz plain chocolate, chopped
50g/2oz/4 tbsp butter, softened
4 size 1 eggs, separated
30ml/2 tbsp rum or brandy (optional)
pinch of cream of tartar
chocolate curls and chocolate-coated
* coffee beans, to decorate*

For the coffee sauce

600ml/1 pint/2½ cups milk
9 egg yolks
60ml/4 tbsp caster sugar
5ml/1 tsp vanilla essence
15ml/1 tbsp instant coffee powder,
* dissolved in 30ml/2 tbsp hot water*

Line a 1.2 litre/2 pint/5 cup terrine or loaf tin with clear film, being careful to smooth it evenly.

In a heatproof bowl set over a pan of barely simmering water, melt the chocolate for 3–5 minutes, then stir until melted and smooth. Remove the bowl from the pan and quickly beat in the softened butter, egg yolks, one at a time, and rum or brandy, if using.

In a clean, grease-free bowl, use an electric mixer to beat the egg whites slowly until frothy. Add the cream of tartar, increase the speed and continue beating until they form soft peaks, then stiffer peaks that just flop over a little. Stir one-third of the egg whites into the chocolate mixture, then fold in the remaining whites. Pour into the terrine or tin and smooth the top. Cover and freeze until ready to serve.

To make the coffee sauce, bring the milk to a simmer over a moderate heat. Whisk the egg yolks and sugar for 2–3 minutes until thick and creamy, then whisk in the hot milk and return the mixture to the saucepan. With a wooden spoon, stir over a low heat until the sauce begins to thicken and coat the back of the spoon. Strain the custard into a chilled bowl, then stir in the vanilla essence and dissolved coffee and set aside to cool, stirring occasionally. Chill until ready to serve.

Remove the loaf from the freezer according to whether you want it frozen or just cold. To serve, uncover the terrine or tin and dip the base into hot water for 10 seconds. Invert the dessert on to a board and peel off the clear film. Cut the loaf into slices and serve with the coffee sauce. Decorate with the chocolate curls and chocolate-coated coffee beans.

RIPPLED CHOCOLATE ICE CREAM

*Rich, smooth and packed with chocolate, this heavenly ice cream is an all-round-the-world
chocoholics' favourite – and it's so easy to make.*

Serves 4

*60ml/4 tbsp chocolate and
  hazelnut spread*
450ml/³/4 pint/1⅞ cups double cream
15ml/1 tbsp icing sugar, sifted
50g/2oz/5 tbsp chopped plain chocolate
plain chocolate curls, to decorate

Mix together the chocolate and hazelnut spread and 75ml/5 tbsp of the double cream in a bowl.

Place the remaining cream and the icing sugar in a second bowl and beat until softly whipped. Lightly fold in the chocolate mixture with the chopped chocolate until the mixture is rippled. Transfer to a plastic freezer container and freeze for about 3–4 hours, until firm.

Remove the ice cream from the freezer about 10 minutes before serving to allow it to soften slightly. Spoon or scoop into dessert dishes or glasses and top each serving with a few plain chocolate curls.

LUXURY MOCHA MOUSSE

Chocolate and coffee combine beautifully in this dessert – strictly for the grown-ups.

Serves 6

225g/8oz cooking chocolate, chopped
50ml/2fl oz/¹⁄₄ cup espresso or
*   strong coffee*
25g/1oz/2 tbsp butter, cut into pieces
30ml/2 tbsp brandy or rum
3 eggs, separated
pinch of salt
45ml/3 tbsp caster sugar
120ml/4fl oz/¹⁄₂ cup whipping cream
30ml/2 tbsp coffee-flavour liqueur
chocolate-coated coffee beans,
*   to decorate*

Melt the chocolate and coffee in a pan. Remove from the heat and beat in the butter and brandy or rum. In a small bowl, beat the yolks lightly, then beat into the melted chocolate. Cool. In a large bowl, use an electric mixer to beat the whites. Add salt and beat on medium speed until soft peaks form. Increase the speed and beat until stiff peaks form. Beat in the sugar, 15ml/1 tbsp at a time, until the whites are glossy and stiff. Beat 15ml/1 tbsp of whites into the chocolate mixture, then fold the chocolate into the remaining whites. Pour into six dishes and chill for at least 3–4 hours. Beat the cream and liqueur in a bowl until soft peaks form. Spoon into an icing bag and pipe the cream on to the mousses. Decorate each with a chocolate-coated coffee bean.

CHOCOLATE AMARETTO MARQUISE

A 23cm/9in springform cake tin is ideal for this recipe, but for special occasions it is worth taking extra time to line a heart-shaped tin carefully.

Serves 10–12

15ml/1 tbsp vegetable oil, such as groundnut or sunflower
75g/3oz/7–8 amaretti biscuits, finely crushed
25g/1oz/2 tbsp unblanched almonds, toasted and finely chopped
450g/1lb cooking or plain chocolate, broken into pieces or chopped
75ml/2½fl oz/⅓ cup Amaretto liqueur
75ml/2½fl oz/⅓ cup golden syrup
475 ml/16fl oz/2 cups double cream
cocoa powder, for dusting

For the Amaretto cream

350ml/12fl oz/1½ cups whipping or double cream
30–45ml/2–3 tbsp Amaretto liqueur

Lightly oil and base-line a 23cm/9in heart-shaped or springform cake tin, then oil the paper. In a small bowl, combine the crushed amaretti biscuits and the chopped almonds. Sprinkle this mixture evenly on to the base of the cake tin.

Place the chocolate, Amaretto liqueur and golden syrup in a pan over a very low heat. Stir frequently until the chocolate is melted and the mixture is smooth. Allow the mixture to cool until it feels just warm to the touch, about 6–8 minutes.

In a bowl with an electric mixer, beat the cream until it just begins to hold its shape. Stir a large spoonful into the chocolate mixture, then quickly add the remaining cream and gently fold into the chocolate mixture. Pour into the prepared tin and tap it gently on the work surface to release any large air bubbles. Cover the tin with clear film and chill overnight.

To unmould, run a thin-bladed sharp knife under hot water and dry carefully. Run the knife around the edge of the tin to loosen the dessert. Place a serving plate over the tin, then invert to unmould the dessert. Carefully peel off the paper, replacing any crust that sticks to it, and dust with cocoa powder. To serve, whip the cream and Amaretto liqueur until soft peaks form and hand round in a separate bowl.

INDEX